Story Hour

Dedication

To all the luckless suitors who died trying
To scale a slope of glass;
To poor Rapunzel, in her tower sighing,
To Abelard, at Mass;
To Dido, on the headlands, hearing the dying
Sound of the oarlocks' ring;
And little Abishag, into her pillows crying,
Warming an old, cold King. . . .*

*I Kings 1:1–3

Story Hour

by
Sara Henderson Hay

With a Foreword by Miller Williams

The University of Arkansas Press
Fayetteville
1998

02   01   00   99   98   5   4   3   2   1

Designed by Liz Lester

⊗   The paper used in this publication meets the minimum
requirements of the American National Standard for Permanence
of Paper for Printed Library Materials Z39.48-1984.

LIBRARY OF CONGRESS CATALOGING-IN-PUBLICATION DATA

Hay, Sara Henderson.
    Story hour / by Sara Henderson Hay ;
with a foreword by Miller Williams.
        p.   cm.
    ISBN 1-55728-542-X (pbk. : alk. paper)
    I. Title.
PS3515.A9323S85   1998
811'.52—dc21   98-13813
                                      CIP

Thanks are due to the following periodicals in whose pages
some of these poems have appeared: *McCalls* ("Story Hour,"
© 1959 McCall Corporation, and "Syndicated Column,"
© 1961 McCall Corporation), *Saturday Review, The Atlantic
Monthly* ("Juvenile Court," © 1961 The Atlantic Monthly
Company), *The Lyric, Voices,* and *The Kentucky Poetry Review.*

For my sister,
Willa Hay Godfrey

Contents

Story Hour 3

Sequel 4

The Grandmother 5

I Remember Mama 7

The Dragon 8

The Sleeper 1 *(She speaks . . .)* 9

The Sleeper 2 *(He speaks . . .)* 10

Photograph Album 11

The Lost Ones 13

The Builders 14

The Marriage 15

Only Son 16

The Grievance 17

The Name 18

The Bird's Nest 19

The Dog 21

The Worrier 22

Rapunzel 23

Winter's Tale 24

One of the Seven Has Somewhat to Say 25

The Memory 27

Our Town: Police Docket 28

Death of H.D., A Prominent Citizen   29

Local Boy Makes Good   31

Letter to the Town Council   32

Juvenile Court   33

Syndicated Column   35

Dr. S——— Advises a Worried Mother   36

The Investigator   37

Housewife   39

Fairy Godmother   40

Interview   41

The Witch   43

Message to the Vigilantes   44

The Flaw   45

New England Tragedy   47

The Goosegirl   48

The Princess   49

The Bad Fairy   50

The Benefactors   51

The Formula   53

Foreword

From time to time there have been suggestions that the nursery rhymes and fairy tales most of us heard as children are too dark and violent, and that perhaps they should be retold in a gentler fashion that would take the scariness out of them.

This clearly was not in the mind of Sara Henderson Hay when she began, one by one, to recast the old tales. Assuming that there are two sides to all stories, she set about telling us those other sides, and in the telling made the stories marvelously ironic, even scarier than they were, sometimes surprisingly moving, and outrageously funny.

There is genius here, not just in the stories behind the stories, but in the choice of the sonnet for the telling of them. The sonnet is all but a lost treasure in our time, partly because it's exquisitely difficult to write one well. These sonnets come across as so natural, so relaxed, simply so very good that the poet seems almost to have thought in the form.

When readers find their bare selves in these poems, there is such fun in the finding that the truth is taken with a grin and a nod of the head. It's a joy to have available again Sara Henderson Hay's timeless gift to us all, so that a new generation of readers can go with her through the back doors of these old houses we thought we knew so well.

Miller Williams

Story
Hour

Story Hour

He swung the axe, the toppling beanstalk fell.
Hurrah, hurrah for Jack, the self-reliant.
The townsfolk gathered round to wish him well.
Was no one sorry for the murdered Giant?
Did no one, as the news spread far and wide,
Protest the means Jack took to gold and glory:
Guile, trespass, robbery and homicide?
It is not mentioned in the popular story.

Dear child, leave off such queries and suggestions,
And let that gullible innocence prevail
Which, in the Brothers Grimms' and our own time,
Applauds the climber, and ignores the crime.
How requisite to every fairy tale
A round-eyed listener, with no foolish questions.

Sequel

And there, in the Beast's place, stood a handsome Prince!
Dashing and elegant from head to toes.
So they were married, thus the story goes,
And lived thenceforth in great magnificence,
And in the public eye. She christened ships,
Cut ribbons, sponsored Fairs of Arts and Sciences;
He opened Parliament, made speeches, went on trips . . .
In short, it was the happiest of alliances.

But watching him glitter, listening to him talk,
Sometimes the Princess grew perversely sad
And thought of the good Beast, who used to walk
Beside her in the garden, and who had
Such gentle eyes, and such a loving arm
To shield her from the briers, and keep her warm.

The Grandmother

You wouldn't think they'd let me live alone
Away out here in the woods, so far from town,
Old as I am, and winter coming on . . .
Still, I suppose, they've problems of their own.
They send the child sometimes, when it's not too late,
With an extra shawl, and a little basket of food.
I like to watch her skipping through the gate,
Bright as a robin in her pretty red hood.

I get so lonely, at the close of day,
Here by the fire, without a thing to do.
I've even thought of that poor mongrel stray
That skulks around, so miserable and thin.
Next time he scratches, I think I'll let him in,
And give him a warm bed, and a bone or two.

I Remember Mama

The trouble is, I never felt secure.
There we were, crammed into that wretched shoe,
Ragged and cold and miserably poor,
And Mama never knowing what to do.
Most of the time we lived on watery stew,
She couldn't even bake a loaf of bread,
And every night she'd thrash us black and blue
And send the snivelling lot of us to bed.

I used to lie awake for hours, and plan
The things I'd do, when I became a man . . .
And this is why I lurk in darkened hallways,
And prowl dim streets and lonely parks, and always
Carry a knife, in case I meet another
Old woman who reminds me of my mother.

The Dragon

My cavern floor is cluttered with their bones.
I am full fed and weary, and still they come;
Some of them riding, armed and helmed, and some
Trudging along on foot, with slings and stones.
All one. The pebbles bounce, the sword blades shatter.
The lances bend and splinter on my scales.
Not strength, nor skill, nor witch's charm prevails.
Knight, huntsman, clerk, the miller's son; no matter.

That nubile Princess in the tower yonder
Will have a long long time to wait, I think,
Unless through very boredom I should blunder,
Unless for very surfeit I should blink,
And, dozing, court the stroke whose consequence
Makes of some fool a bridegroom, and a prince.

The Sleeper

1

(She speaks . . .)

I wish the Prince had left me where he found me,
Wrapped in a rosy trance so charmed and deep
I might have lain a hundred years asleep.
I hate this new and noisy world around me!
The palace hums with sightseers from town,
There's not a quiet spot that I can find.
And, worst of all, he's chopped the brambles down—
The lovely briers I've felt so safe behind.

But if he thinks that with a kiss or two
He'll buy my dearest privacy, or shake me
Out of the cloistered world I've loved so long,
Or tear the pattern of my dream, he's wrong.
Nothing this clumsy trespasser can do
Will ever touch my heart, or really wake me.

The Sleeper

2

(He speaks . . .)

I used to think that slumbrous look she wore,
The dreaming air, the drowsy-lidded eyes,
Were artless affectation, nothing more.
But now, and far too late, I realize
How sound she sleeps, behind a thorny wall
Of rooted selfishness, whose stubborn strands
I broke through once, to kiss her lips and hands,
And wake her heart, that never woke at all.

I wish I'd gone away that self-same hour,
Before I learned how, like her twining roses,
She bends to her own soft, implacable uses
The pretty tactics that such vines employ,
To hide the poisoned barb beneath the flower,
To cling about, to strangle, to destroy.

Photograph Album

This is the one who climbed a hill of glass;
He almost made it, but he slipped and fell.
And this one leapt a ditch of molten brass,
And this one stormed an ogre's citadel.
This one went searching over the rainbow's rim
For a silver apple, and this one sought a flagon
Filled with the Water of Youth up to the brim.
And here is Daddy, standing on the dragon.

And this one, in the locket, with the flower . . . ?
Oh, just a neighbor boy I used to know
Before my father built that silly tower
And all the suitors came. It's rather dim . . .
He moved away, a long long time ago.
Isn't it funny, I still dream of him.

The Lost Ones

If you had been older, maybe, or stronger,
Or known what berries could be used for food,
You might, with luck, have lived a little longer,
And finally found your way out of the wood.
But all the paths your stumbling feet have taken
Only contrived the further to confuse you.
Lie down, poor children. Know yourselves forsaken.
Whoever brought you here intended to lose you.

No one will find you, where the light is slanted
Through the thick boughs, except some bright-eyed bird
Grown bold because you have not spoken or stirred.
You were the stepchildren whom nobody wanted.
Lost in a darkening world, poor babes, good-night.
Under the drifted leaves sleep sound, sleep tight. . . .

The Builders

I told them a thousand times if I told them once:
Stop fooling around, I said, with straw and sticks;
They won't hold up. You're taking an awful chance.
Brick is the stuff to build with, solid bricks.
You want to be impractical, go ahead.
But just remember, I told them; wait and see,
You're making a big mistake. Awright, I said,
But when the wolf comes, don't come running to me.

The funny thing is, they didn't. There they sat,
One in his crummy yellow shack, and one
Under his roof of twigs, and the wolf ate
Them, hair and hide. Well, what is done is done.
But I'd been willing to help them, all along,
If only they'd once admitted they were wrong.

The Marriage

The King and I are more than satisfied;
It's turned out better than we ever hoped.
He's good to her, she made a lovely bride.
And think how we'd have felt, if they'd eloped!
We're quite aware of what his motives were:
He wanted money, and an easy life,
But in the end we had to humor her,
And all she wanted was to be his wife.

As for that fairy tale she likes to tell
About the Frog who scrambled from the well
And gave her back her ball, all dripping wet,
Then turned into a Prince (that's how they met),
We know he's not a Prince—the point is this:
Our poor romantic daughter thinks he is.

Only Son

I want you all to meet Thomas, my son.
One moment, till I lift my thumb a bit,
Now you can see him better, under it . . .
That's where I keep him. Don't you think I've done
A marvelous job in pruning him so small
Without his feeling any pain at all?
It took, of course, maternal dedication,
A velvet claw, and tireless concentration.

And here he stands, my tiny pride and joy.
We're more like sweethearts than like son and mother;
He'd rather be with me than any other.
He's thirty-seven, but he's still my boy.
He'd sooner die, he says, than hurt or grieve me—
Isn't he darling? And he'll never leave me.

The Grievance

Yes, she's a charming girl; we love her dearly.
She's been with us since both of us were small.
One of the family now, or very nearly,
Though actually we aren't related at all.
She was a foundling, and she wandered in
One winter's dusk, out of the rain and cold.
She keeps our house as neat as a new pin.
My parents say she's worth her weight in gold.

But I've a private grudge that rankles yet,
Try as I may to conquer or ignore it.
And sometimes, when I see her sitting there,
Reading, or sewing, or braiding her bright hair,
The old hurt wakens, and I can't forget
That she ate my porridge, and broke my little chair,
And took my bed. And I won't forgive her for it.

The Name

One of my names, and I have many others,
Is Rumpelstiltskin. Desperate people call
On me for aid, by one's or by another's
Particular approach. I hear them all.
Facing a hopeless task, they cry to me.
I help them if I wish, or as I choose.
I'm sometimes swayed by whim, or flattery,
Or repetition of a phrase they use.

What touches me is that they so believe
A name invoked could have some magic power
To turn the clumsy spindle that they hold
Into a tool to avert the impending hour,
And give *me* credit, when their eyes perceive
What daily chaff and straw they've spun to gold!

The Bird's Nest

My name's Elizabeth. I'm also known
As Elspeth, and as Betsy, and as Bess.
It's nice to be four girls instead of one,
Although occasionally, I must confess,
We get a bit confused. Elizabeth
Is very calm and proper; Bess is, too.
Elspeth's a talker, always out of breath;
And nobody knows what Betsy's going to do.

The trouble is that none of us can say
How many of us are here at any minute.
We found a robin's nest, the other day,
With five blue eggs—we counted carefully—
And each of us took one. And we can't see
How there could possibly be four left in it!

The Dog

I didn't get my bone again today.

She went to the cupboard, and the cupboard was bare.

Not even some cereal and a tin of tea

Or a can or two of soup—just nothing there.

I don't mind for myself. I can get by

Scrounging for scraps around the neighborhood,

A couple of tarts, or bits of blackbird pie,

Some cold pease-porridge, nine days old, but good.

It's her I worry about. She's all alone

Except for me; the children both have gone.

And last night, in the kitchen, suddenly

As I was sitting there beside her knee

Down to the table she bowed her poor gray head

And under her breath "Oh God . . . Oh God . . ." she said.

The Worrier

I can't help being just a bit uneasy . . .
Although he hasn't actually implied
That I've been uncooperative, or lazy,
He's made it clear he isn't satisfied.
I do my best. But how can I compete
With Midas? And there ought to be a law
Against a talking mule like Bricklebrit,
Or millers' daughters, spinning it out of straw.

One golden egg a day, it seems to me,
Of solid, genuine, twenty-four-carat stuff,
And laid like clockwork, ought to be enough.
But I've the strangest feeling, like I said,
That things have changed from what they used to be,
And something heavy's hanging over my head.

Rapunzel

Oh God, let me forget the things he said.
Let me not lie another night awake
Repeating all the promises he made,
Freezing and burning for his faithless sake;
Seeing his face, feeling his hand once more
Loosen my braided hair until it fell
Shining and free; remembering how he swore
A single strand might lift a man from Hell. . . .

I knew that other girls, in Aprils past,
Had leaned, like me, from some old tower's room
And watched him clamber up, hand over fist. . . .
I knew that I was not the first to twist
Her heartstrings to a rope for him to climb.
I might have known I would not be the last.

Winter's Tale

I come of a long line of honest workers,
Down-to-earth, thrifty, with a scorn for leisure;
And I've no sympathy to waste on shirkers,
Or those who pass the time in idle pleasure.
Vagrants and profligates deserve their fate—
So why should I be troubled to remember
One shivering vagabond who, last November,
Came begging food and shelter at my gate?

He'd spent the summer fiddling and romancing
While decent folk laid in the winter store—
My house is snug and warm, the cupboard's full;
But evenings, somehow, seem so long and dull.
I wonder what they're like: music, and dancing. . . .
I wish I hadn't turned him from my door.

One of the Seven
Has Somewhat to Say

Remember how it was before she came—?
The picks and shovels dropped beside the door,
The sink piled high, the meals any old time,
Our jackets where we'd flung them on the floor?
The mud tracked in, the clutter on the shelves,
None of us shaved, or more than halfway clean . . .
Just seven old bachelors, living by ourselves?
Those were the days, if you know what I mean.

She scrubs, she sweeps, she even dusts the ceilings;
She's made us build a tool shed for our stuff.
Dinner's at eight, the table setting's formal.
And if I weren't afraid I'd hurt her feelings
I'd move, until we get her married off,
And things can gradually slip back to normal.

The Memory

Thank you, I think I'll just take coffee, black.
I never touch desserts; to tell the truth
I have a sort of phobia, dating back
To an unhappy incident of my youth
Some forty years ago, but even today
That moment's vivid when my sisters and I
Went weeping home and heard our mother say,
"What! Lost your mittens? Then you shall have no pie."

We found our mittens later, in the yard,
And got a double helping, as reward.
But somehow I can never feel the same
Towards pie—it's all mixed up with guilt, and blame,
And the long futile struggle for removal
Of the huge weight of mother's disapproval.

Our Town: Police Docket

Fat Georgy Porgy's first upon the list,
Accused by several mothers, it appears,
Of teasing girls, whom he pursued and kissed,
In consequence reducing them to tears.
Next, Johnny Green, hauled up upon the mat
For wanton drowning of a neighbor's cat;
Third, live-stock theft, by Tom, the Piper's Son,
Caught with the piglet when he tried to run.

And last, a most precocious juvenile
Who managed, by coercion, threats, or guile,
To lure a poor black sheep into a shady
Contract to siphon off the three-bag gain:
One for the Boss, one for the old lady,
And one for the little gangster down the lane.

Death of H.D.,
a Prominent Citizen

You can't tell *me* it was an accident.
Somebody did him in, I'll bet my hat.
Someone sneaked up behind him, where he sat
Dangling his heels, and pushed, and down he went.
It's one of those senseless crimes you read about,
Where there's no clue, no motive, nothing at all
To help the Police. Nobody saw the fall.
But it was murder, not a shred of doubt.

The town's in mourning, lamp-posts draped in black.
The bells will toll, there'll be a big parade.
But all the King's Cavalry and all his men
Marching in ordered ranks won't bring him back;
Nor all the Law Enforcement speeches made
Build up our shattered confidence again.

Local Boy Makes Good

I hear he's changed a lot since he's been grown.
You'd never know him now; but I recall
He used to be so timid and so small
He'd hardly dare to call his soul his own.
I guess we bullied him, but who'd have thought
That he'd be rich and famous, one fine day?
And handsome, into the bargain, so they say.
I don't begrudge him anything he's got,

But all the same, I'd rather like to remind him
That though we're proud of him, and wish him luck,
Here in the poultry yard he left behind him
He'll always be that scrawny little duck,
All bones and pinfeathers and yellow fuzz,
Who couldn't tell you who his father was.

Letter to the Town Council

Dear Sirs: We understand a delegation
Of irate citizens has made demands
That you, the Council, place in expert hands
Control of Hamelin's rodent population.
As owners of a local corporation,
The Acme Trap and Pesticide Supplies,
We find such action hasty and unwise,
And beg you to review the situation.
(And, by the way, a number of physicians
And merchants offer similar petitions.)

Some children have been bitten, it is true,
Some cats and dogs attacked, some housewives scared,
But such complaints can hardly be compared
With loss of jobs and drop in revenue,
Which any business man will realize
Must surely follow, Sirs, if you determine
To interfere with Private Enterprise,
And rid the town of necessary vermin.

Juvenile Court

Deep in the oven, where the two had shoved her,
They found the Witch, burned to a crisp, of course.
And when the police had decently removed her,
They questioned the children, who showed no remorse.
"She threatened us," said Hansel, "with a kettle
Of boiling water, just because I threw
The cat into the well." Cried little Gretel,
"She fussed because I broke her broom in two,

And said she'd lock up Hansel in a cage
For drawing funny pictures on her fence . . ."
Wherefore the court, considering their age,
And ruling that there seemed some evidence
The pair had acted under provocation,
Released them to their parents, on probation.

Syndicated Column

Dear Worried: Your husband's actions aren't unique,
His jealousy's a typical defense.
He feels inadequate; in consequence,
He broods. (My column, by the way, last week
Covered the subject fully.) I suggest
You reassure him; work a little harder
To build his ego, stimulate his ardor.
Lose a few pounds, and try to look your best.

As for his growing a beard, and dyeing it blue,
Merely a bid for attention; nothing wrong with him.
Stop pestering him about that closet, too.
If he wants to keep it locked, why, go along with him.
Just be the girl he married; don't nag, don't pout.
Cheer up. And let me know how things work out.

Dr. S—— Advises
a Worried Mother

Madame, your little girl's extreme aversion
To curds and whey, a common nursery dish,
Stems, we believe, from her unconscious wish
To punish you for some assumed incursion
Upon her ego. Loss of appetite,
Irrational complaints of sudden fright,
Suggest deep-seated feelings of aggression
Which discipline denies overt expression.

Of course the child's stubborn reiteration
That while she was at lunch a large black spider
Quite unexpectedly sat down beside her
Is much too trite and simple an explanation.
We'll do some probing, through analysis,
And find out what her trouble really is.

The Investigator

It's unprovoked and wanton cruelty.
In the first place, the unfortunate mice were blind.
They couldn't have chased her, since they couldn't see
Which way to jump. And secondly, what kind
Of woman is she, to take a carving knife
And maim them so? I never saw a more
Pitiful spectacle in all my life
Than those three tails, limp on the bloody floor.

Maybe she likes to hear things run and squeak . . .
But if it's really *mice* she hates like that
She could set traps, or keep a hungry cat.
There's more in this, perhaps, than meets the eye.
Her husband's not been seen since Monday week.
I think I'll stop by the farm and find out why.

Housewife

No wonder she felt submerged, and put upon,
With such a husband, and those swaggering boys
Up every morning at the crack of dawn,
Strutting around and making all that noise,
(Whatever it was *they* had to crow about,
While she was scratching for their daily ration,
Worrying about the nest egg). I've no doubt
She simply reached a point of sheer frustration.

I'll never forget it to my dying day:
Here she came, flying down the street, and squalling,
"Look out! Look out! Look out! The sky is falling!"
I only hope, before they put her away,
For once in her life, at least, the poor thing knew
Hers was the voice that everyone listened to!

Fairy Godmother

I wonder why they're never satisfied.
One wish should be enough. I give them three.
What's the result? Almost invariably
They squander the first on greed and reckless pride,
The second goes to bolster up the first,
Or add some crowning folly to the sum;
Then with the third the whole thing is reversed
To bring them back to where they started from.

What fools (I quote) these mortals be! It's strange,
They never ask for wisdom, or for truth,
They ask for gold, or power, or revenge,
Unfading beauty, or eternal youth.
I sometimes think I'll cease all dispensations
And leave them to work out their own salvations.

Interview

Yes, this is where she lived before she won
The title Miss Glass Slipper of the Year,
And went to the ball and married the king's son.
You're from the local press, and want to hear
About her early life? Young man, sit down.
These are my *own* two daughters; you'll not find
Nicer, more biddable girls in all the town,
And lucky, I tell them, not to be the kind

That Cinderella was, spreading those lies,
Telling those shameless tales about the way
We treated her. Oh, nobody denies
That she was pretty, if you like those curls.
But looks aren't everything, I always say.
Be sweet and natural, I tell my girls,
And Mr. Right will come along, some day.

The Witch

It pleases me to give a man three wishes,
Then trick him into wasting every one.
To set the simpering goosegirl on the throne,
While the true princess weeps among the ashes.
I like to come unbidden to the christening,
Cackling a curse on the young princeling's head,
To slip a toad into the maiden's bed,
To conjure up the briers, the glass slope glistening.

And I am near, oh nearer than you've known.
You cannot shut me in a fairy book.
It was my step you heard, mine and my creatures',
Soft at your heel. And if you lean and look
Long in your mirror, you will see my features
Inextricably mingled with your own.

Message to the Vigilantes

I'm worried about the boy who minds the sheep—
Oh, not the one in the blue overalls
Who's always sneaking off and going to sleep,
I mean the little nervous one, who calls
For help when nothing's wrong. He isn't fooling.
I think he's genuinely scared to death.
He says he's positive he's heard them howling,
He swears he's seen their footprints on the path. . . .

I know there've been no wolves around for years;
I know that all you men have more to do
Than answer false alarms to soothe his fright . . .
But even so, if anybody hears
The poor child scream again, won't someone go,
Just to be sure that everything's all right?

The Flaw

My wife is beautiful beyond compare.
Her cheek is smoother than the rose's heart;
Her hair's spun silk, her lips a work of art,
Moreover, she's as good as she is fair.
Gentle, unselfish, chaste—she's all of them.
And, in addition, she's extremely rich.
The only trouble is, some stupid witch
Has told her that her every word's a gem.

In consequence, we've rubies by the peck,
Rooms full of sapphires, blue as skies down south,
Bushels of emeralds, and the floor's knee-deep
In diamonds, but I don't get any sleep.
And if she doesn't shut her pretty mouth,
One of these days I'm going to wring her neck.

New England Tragedy

There never was a man with less ambition.
All that he cared about was boats, and nets,
While she was always worrying about debts,
Forever trying to better their condition.
He never seemed to have the slightest notion
That any woman could want more from life
Than what she had, being a trawler's wife,
Stuck in that dingy hovel by the ocean.

It's not surprising that they finally found her
Out where the tide comes pouring over the ledge,
Down on her knees there at the water's edge,
Babbling about some kind of talking fish
Her husband caught, that really wasn't a flounder,
But a Fairy Prince, who was going to grant her a wish.

The Goosegirl

Although on silk and eiderdown I lay,
I never had so comfortless a bed.
As for that minstrel, send the fool away
Before I break his lute over his head.
I will not put another silly stitch
In this fine seam for all the castles in Spain.
I wish I'd never seen the meddling witch
Who changed me from a goosegirl to a queen.

Alas, my darling flock—while I lie late,
Who drives you early to your pebbled streams?
Who brings you home at dusk across the drowsy
Meadows, and past the grove where used to wait
A dark-eyed boy who knows some better games
Than Thimble Thimble, or Ring Around the Rosy?

The Princess

I'll ask for a red rose blossoming in the snow,
A music box hid in a walnut shell;
Nine golden apples on a silver bough,
A mirror that can speak, and cast a spell.
I'll send them East of the moon, and West of the sun,
For a wishing ring made of a dragon's claw . . .
And they will fail, just as the rest have done,
And I can stay at home, with dear Papa.

Oh sometimes in my silken bed I wake
All of a shiver, and my hair on end,
Because again the terrible dream occurred:
What if one of those suitors should come back
With the impossible trophy in his hand,
And I should have to keep my foolish word!

The Bad Fairy

Of course, the King *did* break his promise to me,
(A habit not uncommon with royal blood)
And failed to honor certain payments due me
For spells and charms around the neighborhood.
Moreover, he forgot about the Queen's
Pricking her finger with the darning needle . . .
But those were not the reasons, by any means,
I stole the sleeping baby from the cradle.

It wasn't revenge I wanted, nor useless gold,
Nor out of spite to make the mother weep;
Nor even to punish the father for his pride—
But a warm, human thing to love and hold
As if it were my own, torn from my side;
As if, almost, I had a soul to keep.

The Benefactors

Do not delude yourself that they are kind,
Or think for a single moment they forget
The terms of the agreement—they'll remind
The unfortunate debtor of his reckless debt.
The Miller's conniving Daughter will regret
Her deal with Rumpelstiltskin; and the King
Who promised the Witch to forfeit the first thing
That greeted his safe home-coming will be met

At the gate by his dearest child. Be very sure
Whenever you bargain for your heart's desire,
That whether in sober fact or fairy tale
Grimms' Law of Payment in Full will still prevail.
If not today, then certainly tomorrow,
As many a man discovers, to his sorrow.

The Formula

It isn't easy, being the ugly one,
Or an orphan with the cruelest of stepmothers,
Or a foundling, or the dull-witted youngest son
Competing with eleven brilliant brothers.
But if you've a magic stone, or a wishing ring
Some old crone gave you for helping her cross the road,
And if you follow the rules in everything,
And if you're kind, and don't mind kissing a toad,

You'll scale the slope that nobody else could climb
And kill whatever giant disputes your way,
And reach the impossible goal in record time,
And win the bride or the groom, as the case may be.
For this is the formula which never fails.
(At least, that's how it works in fairy tales.)

About the Author

A recipient of the 1951 Edna St. Vincent Millay Memorial Award and the 1960 Pegasus Award, Sara Henderson Hay published several books of poetry, including *A Footing on This Earth: New and Selected Poems* (Doubleday, 1966), *The Stone and the Shell* (University of Pittsburgh Press, 1959), and *The Delicate Balance* (Charles Scribner's Sons, 1951). She died in 1987.